Teachers, Teams
&
Tugboats

Leadership Lessons from a Life in Global Logistics

By

Rich Higgins

This is a work of non-fiction. While every effort has been made to ensure accuracy, the author makes no guarantees and disclaims liability for errors or omissions.

Contents

Introduction

This book discusses the significance of superior leadership, engaged mentors, and team building. It also conveys the level of personal commitment required by each of us to reach our goals of professional development. These two virtues, personal commitment and professional guidance, are necessary to achieve success in our careers. The book reveals some of the diverse challenges I had to address during my career. Fortunately, my dedicated and thoughtful teachers in the field of Global Logistics were alongside me.

Global Logistics covers all aspects of the supply chain, including ocean and air freight, customs brokerage, duties and tariffs, consolidation, DC operations, e-commerce, trucking, rail, small parcels, and more. The global supply chain has been a prominent topic of interest, especially over the past few years. COVID was a factor in bringing focus to supply chain visibility, spotlighting port congestion, production delays overseas, ocean container backlogs, union work rule issues, rail delays, and ultimately, consumer frustration.

After enduring endless ocean container price hikes and nonsensical, overpriced tariffs, these skyrocketing costs are being forced onto importers, increasing landed costs and causing store closures, bankruptcies, escalating prices, and inflation. We are now responsible for adapting to new sourcing strategies to ship products out of Asia. These volatile supply chain issues have made national news more over the past few years than most other topics, and they have seldom, if ever, been portrayed in a positive light.

After four decades in Global Logistics, I am finishing up my final gig, with the hope that this book will provide others with guidance to help them deal effectively with the challenges and frustrations they will face during their careers. We also need to emphasize the importance of embracing each moment with the seriousness and humor it deserves. We can never take ourselves too seriously. Savor the moment and embrace the challenge. Time passes quickly, so relish every second of this ever-changing journey.

I will shine a bright light on the importance of the profound relationships developed over many years, highlighting those who have pushed, steered, and propelled my career in the right direction, ensuring a safe and productive landing. These dedicated mentors differ in style and delivery but are identical in their commitment to helping me grow during the journey. Like tugboats, these executives can be taken for granted, mostly because of time and distance. However, we should never forget them because they helped make us who we are today. Because of their contributions to us, we can now make our own positive impact on others. This book is dedicated to them.

"As we express our gratitude, we must never forget that the highest appreciation is not to utter their words, but to live by them."

- John F. Kennedy

Chapter 1
Importance of Tugboats

Can you imagine having a global supply chain without tugboats? A tugboat is a small, powerful marine vessel responsible for moving massive container ships, barges, and oil platforms into and out of crowded harbors, narrow channels, and other difficult-to-reach berths. They are mandatory at ports both domestically and internationally.

The first tugboat was built in 1807 by William Symington in Scotland. Currently, there are over 5,600 prodigious container ships operating globally, carrying more than 293 billion metric tons in over 5 million TEUs. It is not an overstatement to say that without tugboats, the entire maritime world would come to a halt. Tugboats are responsible for the following:

- They move large vessels and barges by towing, pushing, or guiding.

- They assist large vessels through channels or with docking and mooring.

- They move rigs and equipment that do not propel themselves.

- Tugboats act as icebreakers and carry firefighting equipment.

- They are small but powerful boats due to their structural engineering and propulsion systems.

- Tugboats provide safe landings and departures for vessels, preventing damage to both the vessel and the port.

- Everything a tugboat does is positive, helping another achieve something it could never have achieved without assistance.

In business, there is a relatively small percentage of senior executives who possess the attributes, patience, and willingness to perform like a tugboat. If you are fortunate, you may have a couple of them guiding you over the course of your career. If you are truly blessed and lucky, you will have more. I worked with seven influential teachers and mentors throughout my career. In the next few chapters, I will share their selfless qualities that deeply impacted me.

Chapter 2
Leaders and Mentors

"One of the greatest values of mentors is the ability to see ahead what others cannot see and to help them navigate a course to their destination." - John C. Maxwell

It is fitting to use the Tugboat as a metaphor for a great leader and mentor. Without Tugboats, the global supply chain as we know it would cease to exist. The same applies to our careers, without these influential executives in our lives, our careers could have been suppressed at best and completely ruined at worst.

We often do not fully appreciate them until they have moved on. Eventually, their true value will shine through, even if you no longer work together. It is never too late to let them know how much you appreciate what they did for you during your career. The best time to tell them is sooner rather than later. This applies to your personal life as well as your professional life.

The best leaders never take themselves too seriously and often have a great sense of humor. My biggest regret was my inability to tell one of my early mentors how much I appreciated him before he passed away unexpectedly. You can avoid the pain I felt for "missing the boat." Take the time to express your gratitude to those who made your journey easier. This book is my way of helping achieve that goal.

It is also important to acknowledge those other (non-mentor) industry colleagues and co-workers who had very positive influences on our careers. Conversely, we also need to identify the negative attributes of others who represent the antithesis of collaboration, support, and business ethics. Let us categorize these executives as follows:

- **Tugboats:** Most commonly, these are our former bosses. In retrospect, these key leaders are the most important and influential executives in our careers. They provided guidance, support, and positive reinforcement when needed for us to succeed. They promote teamwork, personal development, and collaboration as a rule. They are the "best of the best" in our careers.

- **Captains:** The person lawfully in command of a vessel. "Captain" is an informal title of respect given to the commander of a naval vessel regardless of formal rank. In this book, he is a collaborative business colleague who is the leader of a company or a person of influence in the business of global logistics. Examples include senior executives with ocean carriers, air freight companies, trucking firms, or international forwarders who work to promote best practices in your supply chain.

- **Crew Members:** These are our special co-workers or peers within our company who were also committed to excellence and responsible for helping us achieve our goals and objectives. These are co-workers we remain in contact with forever, and some we will bring with us when we move to a new job.

- **Pirates:** Unfortunately, not all bosses are Tugboats. Pirates are the antithesis of positive reinforcement and collaboration. The definition of a pirate is extensive: looter, plunderer, robber, desecrator, destroyer, saboteur. In business, a pirate is someone in power who can effortlessly destroy a culture, wreck a business, desecrate the dignity of workers, and intentionally ruin careers.

I interacted with Pirates up close during my career, and they are usually high-level executives. They are some of the most dangerous people in business, and if possible, should be avoided at all costs. They seem to be more common in privately held, family-owned businesses and are sometimes second-generation, silver-spoon leaders who were handed the business by a parent who built it with minimal help from anyone else. I also worked with a different family-owned company that was a model of ethics and professionalism, vastly different from some loaded with Pirates.

For the record, I am not limiting the terms Tugboats, Captains, Crew Members, and Pirates to just business colleagues. Teachers, coaches, friends, clergy, or others may have positively (or negatively) impacted our lives as well, prior to our business careers. In athletics, especially if you have played multiple sports at different levels, coaches play a major role in our development. One of my high school coaches was a major factor in my life, providing guidance, positive reinforcement, and leadership that adolescents like me needed so badly.

He emphasized the importance of teamwork and selflessness. He insisted that if we worked together in sync, we could beat a team that was more talented than we were. He proved it on a cool October night in the early 1970s, when we beat the #1 ranked team in MA in our division. They averaged 44 points per game, and we were playing on their home field. We entered the game as overwhelming underdogs. When the final whistle blew, this daunting team, on their home field, had been held to only 9 points. We not only won the game; we won the league championship. Years later, after an impressive career, my inspirational coach was honored by being inducted into the MA High School Football Hall of Fame.

Conversely, I had other coaches, both good and bad, with varying degrees of talent and commitment to the players. Regrettably, there were a few who were crude, self-absorbed, demotivating coaches with Napoleon complexes. They were hired because of connections with the head coach, not their coaching or leadership abilities. This quote sums it up quite well:

"A bad leader can take a good staff and destroy it, causing the best employees to flee and the remainder to lose all motivation."

JM Lalonde

Yes, a bad leader (in business or sports) can destroy a company or team, forcing many to leave and causing others to lose all motivation. We see this all the time in both venues. In these situations, we need to disregard and block the negativity of the Pirates and embrace the guidance and respect provided by the true leaders of men we knew. Even these bad experiences can help mold us into better leaders and mentors ourselves. By discarding the bad influences and embracing the motivational strategies of real leaders, we can improve ourselves.

Chapter 3
Early Career

"Energy and persistence conquer all things." Ben Franklin

The first time I had an armed bodyguard, I was 45 years old. I was having dinner in a hotel restaurant in New Jersey with a friend when I never saw it coming. A tall man wearing a suit approached my table and introduced himself. He explained that he was with an executive protection firm that my company had hired to accompany me until the situation was resolved. The issue arose when I was making a trucking change in New Jersey that upset the wrong people. Always a delicate maneuver, I was tasked with adjusting the mix of our carriers, both union and non-union. The changes were not well received and resulted in personal threats. That moment, 23 years after my first day of work, taught me how unpredictable this industry could be. But back when it all began, I was just a 22-year-old with a bachelor's degree and no idea what executive protection even meant. Even during this period of chaos, there were protective leaders guiding me safely through the dilemma.

After graduating from college in the late seventies, my soon-to-be wife and I moved to Boston, where we found a small studio on Commonwealth Avenue and began looking for jobs. We had nothing except our degrees and a profound hope that we could find our first job quickly. I was seeking a teaching position that would also allow me to coach sports. That expectation ended when I was offered a position with a large regional LTL carrier in Cambridge. I spent the next several years with this company in positions including engineering, claims, and operations. My key crew members, Tom, Russ, and Ted, provided me with deep insight into the quirks of the LTL industry. I was given a comprehensive overview of trucking operations, as well as a front-row view of the mercurial interactions between the union and management.

I watched history unfold as trucking was deregulated in 1980. When President Carter signed the Motor Carrier Act into law, it was a devastating change to an industry that had been regulated by the federal government since the Interstate Commerce Act of 1887. This legislation significantly diminished the authority of the Interstate Commerce Commission. Before the law, truckers charged the same rates dictated by the federal rate bureaus. The new act prohibited the rate bureaus from interfering with any carrier's right to publish its own rates. There was an expectation to reduce consumer costs by $8 billion and conserve tens of millions of gallons of fuel per year. The law promoted a competitive environment by loosening federal restrictions, opening the door for more carriers to enter the industry. Ten years after the Motor Carrier Act of 1980 was signed, the number of carriers had doubled nationally.

Those who worked in trucking and logistics, like me, during this period acknowledge that the LTL industry was in chaos. Hundreds of long-term legacy trucking companies closed their doors as profit margins dwindled. Customers now held the bargaining chips, dictating pricing instead of truckers or government rate bureaus. The influx of new non-union truckers changed the game, gaining an edge over carriers deeply entrenched with the union. Work stoppages and strikes became more prevalent as trucking companies struggled to negotiate contract terms. As a result, many retailers modified their dependency on unionized carriers.

My company was a stellar union carrier, providing overnight delivery to and from all six New England states and parts of New York. Our operational execution was a model of excellence for all regional LTL carriers in the U.S. It was my first job after college, and it gave me a trucking perspective that very few logistics executives have prior to moving to the retail sector. It also allowed me to witness history as the Motor Carrier Act of 1980 transformed trucking as we knew it. I watched truckers struggle to adapt to the new deregulated environment. Although I appreciated the teamwork and friendships I developed, especially with Tom, Russ, and Ted, I was eager to make the transition to retail.

Chapter 4
Retail Logistics

"I've learned that people will forget what you said, people will forget what you did, but people never forget how you made them feel."
- Maya Angelou

Bob was my first Tugboat. He was a calm, intelligent mid-level executive in a large, well-known publicly held retailer. He was a breath of fresh air, considering I had just come from a loud, fractious trucking environment that pitted management against the union daily. Yelling was the norm, since we could barely hear each other on the dock over the diesel engine tractors spewing exhaust while multiple forklifts slammed from the dock onto the floors of the trailers being loaded and unloaded. Bob gave me the biggest break of my career at a time I needed it most. After working multiple shifts for years and seldom seeing my family, he hired me into a management position with normal working hours.

Bob was different from previous bosses I had. He always looked me in the eye when he spoke to me, and if an issue needed elaboration, he was never short-tempered. Adopting his demeanor became a great learning tool for me. Bob was a kind, patient executive who had built an excellent team of talented young logistics professionals spread across the country. When we were all in town for business, Bob would invite his team to his home in

Scituate, MA, where you could smell the fresh ocean air from his porch. We really bonded as a team, and we always looked forward to spending time together. I thrived in the new environment, and Bob personally taught me how to use my new company-owned Apple computer. Computers were still in their infancy, but Bob was way ahead of his time. With five regional distribution centers in the network, all five transportation departments were given connectivity that allowed Bob to have a centralized overview of transportation costs, deliveries, freight payment, chargebacks, and weekly reporting.

There was another key crew member directly involved in my hiring and development in addition to Bob. Tom was my best friend in the business world. He endorsed my efforts to change from trucking to retail. We had worked together in trucking before he changed jobs and joined his new boss, Bob. We maintained contact after Tom left, and he made a concerted effort to have me join his new company. He convinced Bob that I had the potential to make a key contribution to their company. I was brought in as an assistant manager, reporting to Tom. Within a year, Tom vacated his position, which allowed me to be promoted to Regional Manager, reporting to Bob, while Tom accepted a role with the company Private Fleet. It was an important step in my development, and I was very appreciative of the new responsibility.

Shortly after my promotion at age 31, with a company that was referred to at the time as "the darling of Wall Street," I lost my license for 30 days due to a DUI. I was driving erratically and was pulled over. Drinking after work with co-workers on this night turned out to be the worst decision of my young career. This mistake crippled me emotionally. I was distraught. I had let my family down; I was embarrassed and disappointed in myself to the point of a depression so severe that it was difficult to get out of. Personally, I was a mess; professionally, I feared this disaster would ruin my career.

There were no remote or hybrid options in the 1980s. I had to be at the office every day, especially because of my new position. Taking 30 days off was not an option. My office was 40 miles southeast of my home, an 80-mile round trip daily. The situation seemed like a bad dream. There were no Ubers in the 1980s, and I could not afford a daily 80-mile round-trip taxi service. I was in a dilemma that seemed unsolvable.

The outlook was dismal; I had no options at my disposal until an angel unexpectedly showed up at my home with a solution. He told me not to worry and that he would personally drive me to and from work each day until I could drive again. The angel was my previously mentioned friend, Tom. He offered to pick me up in my town (15 miles from his home) before going to work, which increased his normal daily round trip to work from his home from 60 miles to 110 miles. And there were no strings attached. He did this solely to help a friend in need.

I was stunned by this selfless act of kindness. As a learning experience, I promised myself to "pay it forward" whenever I had the opportunity to do something similar for someone else in need. Tom accepted nothing, even though I tried to offer gas, coffee, lunch, and money. The only thing he wanted was for me to be able to continue working and support my young family. And for the record, Tom also had two children. He was making this sacrifice to help a friend. I will always be indebted to my buddy for saving my career during this period of my life. He taught me the importance of compassion in business, an attribute seldom seen in that world.

"Remember that mentor leadership is all about serving."- Tony Dungy

When I returned to work, the management support was overwhelming. Reminding me of the song *"Wind Beneath My Wings,"* the positive reinforcement and teambuilding exhibited by my co-workers was uplifting and sincere. I was appreciative of the support and continued to thrive in that environment. In retrospect, it was a textbook example of how a company can support an employee who has fallen on tough times. I immediately refocused on the present and performed to the best of my abilities.

Within two short years, Bob promoted me again, this time to his own position, overseeing all five regional offices (Chicago, NYC, Atlanta, and two in MA), as he moved into a new job. With the support of his peers, he bypassed several more tenured internal applicants when he selected me, and I was fully committed to not letting him down. It was during a period of aggressive expansion, opening two additional distribution centers in Pennsylvania and Florida. These new regional facilities would supplement the others we already had. Most of the engineering and design of the buildings were done in-house by our IT team. DC Operations shifted key managers to run the new facilities to ensure a smooth transition. My team and I spent months on the road setting up the regional offices. The collaboration and execution displayed by our entire division were commendable. Both "go-live" dates were met with few, if any, start-up issues in either Florida or Pennsylvania.

A few years later, the company was acquired by another retailer. Once the fifth largest discount retailer in the country, we were all devastated. Our logistics and distribution teams were, in my opinion, the best group of industry talent in the country. Starting at the manager level and ending with the Senior Vice President, we had a plethora of highly marketable talent. Even today, many of my colleagues are still employed and highly respected, while others retired with very successful careers at fine companies. I will always cherish my time with this group. I was entrusted with significant responsibility, learned an incredible amount, and was very marketable at age 35. I am especially thankful to Bob and Tom for their dedication to me. Their focus on professional development, trust, and teams put me on the right track early in my career.

At this early stage, I was not very familiar with the term "recruitment," but this was, in fact, the first time I was actively recruited by another company. This meant a company was proactively trying to hire me, versus me sending a bunch of resumes out to multiple companies. I felt humbled that they reached out to me. During my tenure at my last company, I developed an excellent relationship with an industry "captain." Norm was the CEO of a multi-faceted New Jersey-based trucking company. His company provided truckload, LTL, and pool distribution services to the tri-state area of New York, New Jersey, and Pennsylvania. He was also an existing business partner with my future boss, who was trying to fill a key position in a major footwear company.

Chapter 5
The Teacher

"The mediocre teacher tells. The good teacher explains. The superior teacher demonstrates. The great teacher inspires."
- John Crawford Crosby

Charlie was a brilliant executive with a large footwear company in the Boston area. He had a magnetic personality and held dual roles as SVP of both Human Resources and DC Operations. He was passionate about business and focused on introducing operational efficiencies in the DC while simultaneously reducing all kinds of costs, both operational and freight. Charlie also had a great sense of humor, blending his quick wit with anecdotes about his peers, his family, and members of the DC and Traffic teams.

Charlie and I hit it off immediately, partly because, like me, he was also the proud father of two young daughters, and we were similar in other ways as well. Although we connected immediately, Charlie was not easy to work for. Corporate pressures added layers of complexity that he and the other senior executives had to manage. He was highly demanding, constantly juggling a long list of priorities that required my full attention and were time-consuming. I traveled out of state almost the entire first year we worked together.

My primary goal was to reduce freight costs, enhance our business relationships with all service providers, and identify viable "pool distribution" operators for all states east of the Mississippi, including all states from Maine to Florida. I was also tasked with reducing our dependency on unionized carriers and shifting more volume to lower-cost, non-union providers. This was not an easy task, as unions, particularly the Teamsters, were actively trying to expand at that time. Random local strikes, as well as some highly visible national strikes by major LTL carriers, including Yellow Freight and Consolidated Freightways, added further challenges.

Our antiquated DC sortation system segregated stores only by region or state, not by individual store. As a result, we built "shotgun" or "fluid loaded" (mixed) trailers that required rehandling, de-segregation, and delivery by local truckers. A specialized trucking provider was needed for this business, and it was my responsibility to travel state to state to identify, meet, and implement the most viable carriers.

The importance of my role became crystal clear when I learned that my company would likely be filing for Chapter 11 bankruptcy to reorganize its debt while continuing operations and providing a structured process to repay vendors over time. I immediately realized the critical nature of Charlie's assignment: I was on a mission to significantly reduce transportation costs to help lower overall corporate operational costs. This was necessary for the company to survive and quickly emerge from bankruptcy. I understood how vital my efforts were and how delicate our business relationships were with hundreds of vendors, truckers, and service providers.

The sobering reality was that many of our key business partners could be financially hurt by prepetition debt that might not be fully reimbursed, or possibly not at all. Any vendor invoices not paid by the Chapter 11 filing date would be held in abeyance as the court conducted its review. It was up to me to maintain those business relationships and ensure our supply chain remained intact during the bankruptcy announcement. I had to assure vendors that post-petition payments (all invoices submitted after the filing date) would be guaranteed while pre-petition debts were reviewed by the courts. Most vendors continued their partnerships with us, although a few did not.

Within about six months, we emerged from bankruptcy, and most vendors received partial reimbursement of their prepetition debt, which was better than the alternative. This experience was an important business lesson. Successfully filing for bankruptcy, and then emerging from it, is uncommon. It would never have been achieved without our logistics team working closely and collaboratively with Charlie and our senior executives to ensure there were no supply chain breakdowns and that products flowed perfectly from origin to destination.

Charlie had built a solid logistics team of seasoned DC, transportation, and IT talent. Before he moved into retail, he had been a teacher, and he applied those skills in his dual executive roles. Like most companies, we had a small group of "A players" and a slightly larger group of mediocre performers; some lost their jobs during the bankruptcy. During the turnaround, I had a frank conversation with Charlie about the talent level in our logistics team. I felt there were a few managers "not cutting the mustard" or living up to expectations.

I asked him, "How can you tolerate some of the slower-moving, less engaged managers and maintain your composure?" I will never forget his thoughtful response:

"Rich, it would be easy to fire all the B and C players and replace them with A players, but I see it as a challenge to myself to use my teaching skills to help them improve. Everyone is driven by something, it is my job to find what motivates that person. If I can make a C player a B player, or a B player a B-plus, then I have done my job. If I cannot do that, I am not doing a good job."

I remembered that response for the next 30 years and did my best to adopt his wisdom. Unfortunately, business conditions sometimes do not allow time for improvement, and termination becomes necessary. Nonetheless, these words of wisdom remain invaluable: as Charlie eloquently stated, "We are not only bosses, we are teachers."

"If your actions inspire others to dream more, learn more, do more, and become more, you are a leader." - John Quincy Adams

Speaking of talent, I worked closely with a talented "crew manager" who was well-versed in both DC operations and IT connectivity. Gary was a motivated "A player" with the most professional business demeanor of anyone I have met in my career. He was knowledgeable in all aspects of DC operations and systems and a pleasure to work with. Gary could easily and effectively communicate with all levels, including the C-Suite, DC associates, peers, his direct reports, and his boss, all in a measured, comforting tone. Every executive should be as fortunate as I was to have a "Gary" during their career. His personality countered mine, and his expertise, especially in IT, offset my lack of knowledge in that area. Our strengths complemented each other, and together we were a strong team. We could not have achieved what we did, pre- and post-bankruptcy, without his focused expertise and talent.

Some executives like to be the smartest person in the room and may not embrace others' expertise because of ego. The best leaders understand both their strengths and areas needing improvement and have no hesitation in hiring people who might be smarter than them in certain areas. Both parties' benefit, creating a win-win relationship. Gary helped me become a better executive, and I believe I helped him grow as well, thanks to the mutual admiration and trust we shared.

Chapter 6
The Merger

Great difficulties may be surmounted by patience and perseverance.
-Abigail Adams

Gary and I worked together through additional business challenges, such as the merger with another major MA-based footwear company. This merger would literally double the size of my company to over $1 billion. It involved the physical transfer of their distribution center to our larger DC and, eventually, the implementation of a new, sophisticated WMS (Warehouse Management System) that would replace our antiquated multilevel carousel sortation system. Working with operations, transportation, and our dedicated truckers, we transferred over five hundred 53' trailers over a three-day weekend, emptying their entire building. With the entire shoe inventory now in one location instead of two, we had the flexibility to reallocate both exempt and non-exempt manpower to meet the needs of the newly consolidated distribution center.

This was the second company merger I went through in six years. The process is quite interesting, as it involves a due diligence comparison of departments (like Human Resources, IT, Transportation, DC Operations, Buying, Store Operations, etc.) because redundant positions exist in each company and major layoffs are often required. In most cases, the acquiring company selects their own departments when combining with a new company. Fortunately for me, they selected my Transportation department and most of our DC Ops team (including Gary) to run those areas in the newly combined company. This was flattering to my staff and me, but it meant the acquiring company would be laying off some of our colleagues on both sides, a sobering process.

The new alignment resulted in my team taking on additional responsibilities, including international logistics, which was new for us. We embraced the new responsibilities with unbridled enthusiasm. In my opinion, International Logistics (ocean, air, origin consolidation, PO management, customs, etc.) is the most exciting segment of Global Logistics. The best teachers in this area are our colleagues from Asia, including the ocean carriers, port executives, sales executives, and forwarders. Having the pleasure of being with them in Asia, absorbing their unsurpassed knowledge of international logistics and operational excellence, is the greatest gift one can receive.

This job provided me with the most significant learning experiences of my career. I spent time in Asia, specifically China, Hong Kong, and Taiwan. Spending time in China is mandatory for anyone looking to better understand global logistics. I visited factories, had multiple port tours, met with ocean carriers at their headquarters, toured consolidation warehouses, and met a large number of Asia-based logistics executives. Once I visited Asia for the first time, I never wanted to leave. It provides clarity on the supply chain flow of products, from the inception of the PO at the factory all the way to the customer's warehouse.

The comprehensive knowledge of global logistics possessed by executives in Asia is awe-inspiring. Spending quality time overseas early in my career with John, Ron, Endo, and Irene taught me not only impeccable operational and administrative execution but also revealed the depth and breadth of their knowledge and the pride they have in what they do for retailers all over the world. The level of automation and sophistication seen at ports such as Shanghai, Ningbo, Hong Kong, Yantian, and Kaohsiung is vastly superior to any U.S. port. Asian ports embrace automation and sophistication, while unions at U.S. ports often fight automation and attempt to exclude it from contracts to prevent job loss. This lack of forward thinking is most evident when visiting both U.S. and Asian ports. If this mindset continues with the Longshoremen, the U.S. will never be remotely close to the level of port productivity, automation, and operational excellence evident in Asia.

If there is one solid recommendation I can give a young executive looking to better understand global logistics, it is this: take the time to travel overseas and visit Asia to learn from those with world-class knowledge. Most direct importers in retailing have existing offices in Asia, so take advantage of it. It is a learning experience you will cherish for the rest of your life, especially if your career involves the global supply chain.

After working together for five years, I decided to move on to another challenge with a major toy retailer. However, my friendship and business relationship with Gary continued throughout the rest of my career, and he will always be my most talented colleague and crew member.

Chapter 7
Giving Back to the Community and Charities

"A leader is one who knows the way, goes the way and shows the way." - John C Maxwell

Making the singular effort to be successful at your job is not enough in life. Your family is always number one, but embracing your community and contributing to charitable endeavors is a close second. There are hundreds of 501(c)(3) charities across the country that we can consider working with, either directly or through our companies.

I was fortunate to be with a company that was a huge proponent of, and donor to, The Dana-Farber Cancer Institute's Jimmy Fund Walk. This annual walk is the largest single-day walk fundraiser in the nation, taking place every fall. The walk covers the entire 26.2-mile Boston Marathon course. Since 1989, the walk has raised over $185 million for cancer care and research. The funds support both adult and pediatric cancer patients.

In dedication to our many friends and family members who have been affected by cancer, my family and I have supported this charity, raising money for it since its inception. In fact, I have completed 19 Jimmy Fund Walks, 17 of which were the entire 26.2-mile course. What I learned is that no matter how in shape you are, walking 26.2 miles is painful. But when you cross the finish line at Copley Square in Boston, it seems well worth the effort. I can say firsthand how wonderful all the doctors, nurses, and staff members are at the Dana-Farber Cancer Institute.

Be sure to embrace other charities sponsored by your employers as well. Most companies are altruistic, so be supportive when they are doing good for others.

Chapter 8
The Woodworker

"The delicate balance of mentoring someone is not creating them in your own image, but giving them the opportunity to create themselves." - Steven Spielberg

Dave was my next Tugboat, recruiting me away from a footwear retailer to a toy retailer. Dave was a proven, well-respected senior logistics executive for three major retailers, two in the Southeast. He had recently been recruited as the new SVP for a well-known toy retailer in the Northeast. By this time, I was gaining knowledge in all aspects of global logistics, including international contracts and negotiations. I had visited Asia a few times and met with many of the major ocean carriers, port executives, and consolidation companies. Dave was building a new team and asked me to become his Director of Global Logistics. I was happy in my current position, but Dave won me over in our first interview. He was disarmingly frank and stated that he was clueless as far as transportation and logistics were concerned and that he needed my help.

A large, well-respected retail holding company was planning for the toy company to be spun off as a publicly traded company on its own. Prior to the spin-off, the corporate parent negotiated all contractual agreements for its subsidiaries, including this one. My job with the new company was to individually renegotiate all logistics contracts, including ocean, air, LTL, rail, small package, truckload, origin management, and consolidation.

Dave sensed some tension in this new Transportation and Distribution team he had inherited and wanted to set the ground rules upfront. We had to work collaboratively with each other because there was no corporate group overseeing us anymore; we were on our own. In a stroke of genius, when we were all together (about 30 of us) for the first time, he brought everyone in from all DC locations, including AZ, Kentucky, PA, NJ, and MA, and we spent the week with consultants from Aubrey Daniels. AD was (and still is) one of the foremost experts in leadership and workforce motivation. Our topic was R+, discussing positive reinforcement and bringing out the best in people. I will never forget how impressed I was with Dave, who not only talked the talk, he walked the walk. He wanted his team to treat each other with dignity and respect. What a great move by Dave, and what a great experience it was for the rest of us.

There were many skeptics in the company when I initially informed Dave that all the new contracts I would be renegotiating would be lower than the ones negotiated by the prior parent company. Most current executives said they would just be happy if we came in "close to" the prior rates. After all, the previous parent had the negotiating leverage of using the supply chain volume of all six of their subsidiary companies. I think some thought my comments were a mix of cockiness or arrogance, but it was neither.

Within the first year, I pleased Dave by significantly reducing our rates in every contract previously negotiated by the parent. This involved holding several RFPs simultaneously for LTL, truckload, rail, ocean freight, customs brokerage, Asia consolidation, and PO management. The ocean and origin CFS rates were lowered by several million dollars. We imported about 15,000 FEUs (40-foot equivalent units) annually to our five distribution centers. Each container was segregated and floor-loaded at origin for a specific location in Arizona, Kentucky, Massachusetts, Pennsylvania, or New Jersey. Origin CFS fees were reduced by 85%, and ocean rates were lowered between $1,000 and over $3,000 per container.

Having worked for a high-volume importer previously, I was aware of market rates for all modes of transportation. Because of both the bankruptcy and subsequent merger, I was aware of the lowest rate levels and knew how to get them without compromising service levels. Although the process was difficult and painful at times, the bankruptcy and merger process helped my career by forcing me to identify and research the lowest domestic and international rate levels for all modes of transportation. To be honest, the corporate rates with the holding company were well above market.

The primary reason for the above-market rates was due to their total reliance on the ANERA ocean carriers. ANERA stands for Asia North America East Bound Rate Agreement, which was formed under the Shipping Act of 1984. These carriers were the so-called "Tier 1" ocean carriers, and if you used them, you paid a huge premium. There were seven ocean carriers that were members of this conference, and they charged basically the same rates. In addition, there was a large group of second-tier carriers, referred to as the non-conference (or non-cons). Their transit times were slightly longer than ANERA's, but the difference was negligible overall. I had great success using the non-conference carriers previously, so we shifted most of our ocean volume from the overpriced ANERA conference to this lower-cost group.

Not only were the rate levels compellingly lower, they offered generous free time on their containers, sometimes more than 30 days. Free time is an essential benefit in the toy business, as we import 12 months a year but ship out 80% of our annual volume to stores between Black Friday and Christmas. Our distribution centers and third-party warehouses fill to capacity prior to Thanksgiving, so we need as much free time as possible on containers we are unable to unload immediately. If you wanted lower rates with a specific ANERA carrier, you would need to apply for an Independent Action (or IA). We successfully negotiated IAs with some of the top ANERA carriers, which was a huge win for us.

A few years later, the Federal Maritime Commission (FMC) found the ANERA carriers guilty of contract abuse. They lost their operating authority when they violated the 1984 Shipping Act. During the 1998 peak season, many shippers and NVOCCs (non-vessel operating common carriers) were charged a premium ranging from about $400 to over $1,000 per container above the rate levels reflected in their signed contracts. Oddly, the FMC did not fine the ANERA carriers, but the conference and their practices ended. At age 43, I was now developing a confidence that I could walk into any company and identify potential savings throughout its supply chain.

Dave was really funny, but with a kind of warped sense of humor. It was at this time when I was a light smoker, and I would occasionally make the mistake of leaving my package of butts on my desk. Whenever I made this mistake, I would come back to my office, and all the remaining cigarettes had been put through an electric pencil sharpener, with the ground tobacco dumped all over my desk.

On other occasions, he was a little more devious. He gave me this big, beautiful office, and most of my days were comprised of meetings with potential carriers and service providers. One day, I held a large meeting with some trucking executives. After we exchanged business cards, they started to laugh. One of them said, "I guess someone in here does not like you?" One of them handed me my own business card, and Dave had handwritten on each of my business cards the words "shit for brains." He inserted it between my name and my title, and the whole room burst into laughter. Shortly thereafter, Dave walked into the office, asking me if I knew where he had left his pen.

Of course, it was all in good fun, as Dave and I had a great relationship at work and out of the office as well. Dave is also a devout Christian and a world-class woodworker. To this day, he dedicates his weekends to teaching Bible study at his church in Texas. I respected him immensely, both as a person and as a boss. But, like most things in life, we were thrown a curveball out of the blue. At the last minute, before spinning us off, the Holding Company made the decision to "sell us to another retailer" instead of allowing us to be a separate operating company. We had already recruited a plethora of industry talent who had recently moved their families and changed their lives, including my own.

Relocating is a traumatic experience for most families, especially those with teenage girls. At this time, my daughters were 15 and 17, respectively, a soon-to-be freshman and junior in high school. The decision to relocate went over like a lead balloon. They were being uprooted from their lives, leaving their friends and classmates behind.

"You gain strength, courage, and confidence by every experience in which you really stop to look fear in the face. You must do the thing you think you cannot do." - Eleanor Roosevelt

There is nothing more difficult in business than making the decision to accept a position requiring relocation when your children are at the adolescent stage of their lives. It is a truly impressionable time, and they need consistency and balance in their lives. Their hearts were broken, and there was nothing we could say or do to mitigate the situation. It did not matter that we had a new home in a beautiful area of New England, they wanted to go home. Even though it was the best business decision for our family to relocate, the level of empathy we felt for the girls was overwhelming.

We hoped that "time would heal all wounds," as the saying goes, but in this situation, it did not. My older daughter, the junior, adapted well a few months into the school year, but my youngest daughter, the freshman, did not. She became more withdrawn and insular. Unfortunately, each of them seemed comfortable taking out their frustrations on their mom instead of me. To say this period was difficult is an understatement. We did go to some family counseling sessions, which were not as helpful as we had hoped.

Our friends, including my boss Dave and his wife, were supportive and comforting. Those friends with similarly aged kids were the most helpful, though. We realized that, regardless of the situation, adolescent girls between the ages of 15 and 19 go through a brief period when they "reject" or "cast off" their parents. During this period, they believe everything the parent says or does is either wrong, stupid, or both. One of our friends called it the "Planet Neptune Years." He said that although the girls are physically here at home, they are emotionally residing on Neptune for that five-year period. Parents can do nothing right during this time frame, so we need to realize that. At age 19, the problem usually ends because the girls leave home for college. When they are away at college, they suddenly realize how smart and important their parents are, and can continue to receive money every week. My youngest daughter is now 43 years old with four kids (two of them girls). We hope they will not go through a similar experience. For those considering relocating for a new job, do not underestimate the impact it may have on your adolescent children. View the potential move from their perspective with both thoughtfulness and empathy.

The decision by the Holding Company to sell us to another retailer instead of spinning us off as our own company was met with overwhelming disdain. Most of the new team recruited to run the new company would be replaced by the executives at the acquiring company. Most felt they were misled at best and lied to at worst. The honeymoon would soon be over. Going through the normal due diligence process during the merger, it was clear that their DC and store operational philosophies were not consistent with ours. For me, it was another great learning experience because it was the third corporate acquisition I had been involved with in a ten-year period. Sadly, it was clear where this one was heading, and I left the company a few months after Dave. I will always remember the good times and the many successes we enjoyed together in the years we worked together.

Chapter 9
The Voice of Reason

"A good leader leads the people from above them. A great leader leads the people from within them." - M.D Arnold

Now at age 45, I was probably at the highest level of marketability in my career. There were two offers immediately on the table from major retailers, one on the East Coast and the other on the West Coast. Greg, my fourth Tugboat, was the SVP of HR for the East Coast retailer and a close friend of my second Tugboat, Charlie. Both job offers were viable, but the West Coast offer was slightly better. We had some trepidation about relocating again, even though my oldest daughter was now away at college, my other daughter was still in high school. However, this situation was different because we had family in the area we were considering moving to.

I made the decision to accept the West Coast job and advised Greg accordingly. He thanked me and said he would still check in with me every week to make sure my transition was going well. As promised, he did check in weekly, telling me he was keeping my position open in case I changed my mind. After eight weeks, it was clear the move was not as advertised. Benefits, as I understood them, were not being honored, and the sale of my home back East was moving slowly due to market conditions. When Greg called again, I told him I would be joining him, and he was pleased.

It was the best, albeit the most difficult, career decision I ever made. My family was in total disarray, as both girls were adamantly opposed to moving 3,000 miles away. In addition, my wife was having some medical issues, and the West Coast company was unable (or unwilling) to extend medical benefits to her until she moved to California. This was the last straw for me. Greg took care of all loose ends, and I was coming home. I thank God for his persistence, support, and friendship. He was the voice of reason, and keeping the position open for me for two months was both flattering and truly amazing. I am forever grateful to him.

We worked well together during our time together, but the issues were challenging. The company was publicly held and had recently emerged from Chapter 11 bankruptcy. It was now on a good track but had a long way to go. Despite the challenges, it was a great company to work for, the best I had ever worked for. We implemented major changes in the supply chain by introducing a new WMS (Warehouse Management System) and TMS (Transportation Management System) in a short period of time.

The Achilles' heel for the company was that it was highly unionized. Unlike Walmart, Kohl's, and most other department stores, our stores, distribution centers, and truckers were unionized. Inflexible work rules, high costs, and random strikes were the norm. Efforts were made to mitigate reliance on union employees and truckers. The trucking initiative was mine. After successfully changing providers at the home office by shifting about 90% of the work to a non-union carrier, we focused on our second larger DC in New Jersey. This initiative resulted in my first encounter with "executive protection."

The New Jersey changes did not go as smoothly as we hoped. In fact, there were threats made that necessitated a full-time bodyguard. I was with a colleague eating dinner at the hotel restaurant when a tall, well-dressed gentleman introduced himself as my full-time bodyguard, assigned by Greg and our VP of Loss Prevention at corporate. They also provided executive protection to the CEO as a safeguard. They were not taking the threat lightly. For the next ten days, I had someone with me, or nearby, 24/7. When I flew home the next day, he accompanied me to the gate (this was well before the TSA restrictions we have today), and on arrival in Boston, another EP team member was waiting for me and followed me all the way to my home in central Massachusetts. He parked in the turnaround area at the base of my driveway and stayed until I left for work on Monday, after which we reversed the process.

One of the hardest things I ever had to do was explain to my wife and kids that a man would be monitoring our home and every move for an unknown period. I did my best to make it sound innocuous, but they knew it was not normal. Fortunately, teenage girls take very few things seriously, so it did not seem to bother them. But it really worried my wife.

Not knowing anything about executive protection services, I learned a lot and have a great deal of respect for them. Most are former FBI agents or state police. If I recall correctly, the owner of this firm was a former FBI agent. I was told that upon arrival in my town, they notify the local police department and let them know what they are doing. This is because nosy neighbors and friends would not look kindly on an occupied black van situated on my property 24/7. However, I was not aware that they would accompany us everywhere, including the bank, stores, church, and restaurants.

The firm also researched the threat and confirmed it to be valid. We knew who made it, but it seems that person had neither the blessing nor the support within the union to carry out such a threat. After about ten days, I requested that the protection be removed because it was smothering, and I had enough. Greg approved my request, and life returned to relative normalcy. In retrospect, executive protection was a good learning experience.

As great a company and leadership as we had, we could not reach the financial goals set for us. The retail industry at this time was exploding with the unstoppable growth of Walmart, Kohl's, and Target, so we were forced into Chapter 7 liquidation. After 43 years in business, this highly respected regional discount retailer with 10,000 employees was closing its doors. This was a sad day because the company was loaded with some of the best executive talent I had worked with to date. Despite that, we could neither withstand the unionization nor the intimidating competition from comparable retail chains.

Chapter 10
Meet Me in St Louis

"A leader takes people where they want to go. A great leader takes people where they do not necessarily want to go, but ought to be."
- Rosalynn Carter

Shortly after the dust settled with my prior company, I received an exploratory call from a Headhunter based in the Midwest, who was representing a major Midwest-based footwear and apparel retailer. The difference between a Headhunter and a Recruiter is that a Headhunter's approach is targeted primarily at passive candidates who are not actively looking for a job. The jobs they fill are usually very high-level executive positions or specialized, hard-to-fill roles. They are often focused on a specific industry. Conversely, a Recruiter is reactive and broad, managing a pool of active job seekers who are applying for advertised positions. As we spoke on the phone, he was very cautious not to expose the specific company but clearly articulated what he needed from me, as he subjected me to an unending number of pointed questions.

At the end of our phone conversation, he told me that he was not authorized to provide the company with any information about me unless he met me in person. This was about 24 years ago, when there were no Zoom, Google, or Microsoft Teams calls, but I still felt a bit uncomfortable with the comment. Two weeks later, he called asking me to meet him at a restaurant at Logan Airport for lunch so we could continue our conversation. The meeting was professional, but when it ended, I had more questions than answers. He made an odd comment that he would give the company his feedback and my credentials, but he was not sure they would ask me to come to their headquarters for an interview. I figured that was the end of it, c'est la vie!

Surprisingly, he called a few days later, saying they were interested and looking forward to meeting me. The company was a well-respected, multi-billion-dollar footwear retailer, and the position was the #1 Executive in Logistics, whose incumbent was retiring. I flew to their headquarters for a day of interviews with several executives, peers, and potential direct reports. My first interview was with the retiring senior logistics executive, and we immediately bonded. It was a successful visit, and I returned twice more for additional interviews, psychological testing, and a weekend real estate tour with my wife. As it turned out, their CFO had worked with both Charlie and Greg, my first and third mentors. I was told they had struggled for months to find the right person, and I was flattered. This was the job of my dreams, the #1 Logistics position at a thriving, multi-billion-dollar company.

Although we received a generous offer letter, my wife and I still had a degree of trepidation, which primarily involved relocating. This time, however, it was because my father was very ill. I shared this with neither the Headhunter nor the company. As of this writing, there are times I still regret my decision, but I turned the position down. Both sides were truly disappointed in the outcome, but my wife and I felt we made the right decision for that moment. As it turned out, my dad passed away about a month after I turned the position down. I was able to spend some quality time with him the night before he passed away. If I had accepted the job in St. Louis, I would not have been with my father on the last night of his life. I don't think I could have forgiven myself.

Chapter 11
Discard the "Rabbit Ears"

"What you do has far greater impact than what you say"
- Stephen Covey

The best athletes, businessmen, or politicians have thrown away their "rabbit ears." It is a derogatory term meaning the person is easily distracted or can be thrown off their game very easily. In sports, it is a strategy to try to make a basketball player miss an important free throw, a baseball pitcher focus on the comments instead of the batter, or a hockey player in the penalty box lose his cool and disrupt his concentration. The best players and business executives have the discipline to focus on the matter at hand and completely "tune out" negative comments, even if it is the hardest thing they have ever done.

It is inevitable that at some point in your career, you will encounter someone petty, negative, or jealous who will test you with negative comments. There is nothing worse than having a successful career derailed by getting into a juvenile back-and-forth argument with a narrow-minded colleague. In these situations, always rise above the reactionary banter and ignore the other person. Remember, the lion never turns around when the small dogs bark.

Never engage these Pirates; their goal is to ruffle feathers only. Just look at how distorted our current political climate is at the highest level. Even the most innocuous comments or minor criticisms are met with a barrage of demeaning, retaliatory nonsense because the recipient is "thin-skinned." It is not only embarrassing to the small-minded combatants; it is embarrassing to watch as a citizen. Always be professional and maintain decorum, even though some segments of our society fail at it daily. Those who engage in it are not real leaders and never will be. Stay disciplined and never stoop to their level. Remember, it does not matter what anyone says or thinks about you as a person. What is important is how you feel about yourself.

Chapter 12
Be Wary of Pirates

"Obstacles don't have to stop you. If you run into a wall, don't turn around and give up. Figure out how to climb it, go through it, or work around it." - Michael Jordan

We discussed in Chapter 2 the traits of a Pirate in business. As previously noted, the Merriam-Webster dictionary definition of a Pirate is extensive: a looter, plunderer, robber, despoiler, desecrator, destroyer, saboteur. In business, it is someone in power who can effortlessly destroy a culture, wreck a company, desecrate the dignity of workers, and intentionally ruin careers. You need to do everything in your power to avoid these people. However, for family or financial reasons, some may have to endure this abuse for an unspecified period.

I have worked with people like this intermittently over my career, and they are more prevalent in family-owned companies where nepotism is rampant and there is no viable board of directors to rectify offenses. When family members assign other family members or personal buddies to high-level positions for which they are not qualified, only disaster will result. Hiring unqualified candidates to handle multiple roles is even worse. These are the people who usually think they are the smartest in the room, despite their lack of knowledge in the subject matter. I had a boss who was convinced that a 30-minute conversation with a more knowledgeable subordinate would allow him to know as much as that person, even though the subordinate had spent 30 years in the field. These are the most dangerous Pirates, the ones who neither respect the person nor the intricacies of the job.

There was an executive I observed who was both a malignant narcissist and a mean-spirited tyrant. He was not only an abusive, bullying leader; he also had unethical tendencies in his business. He did not invest a dime in the upkeep or modernization of his facilities, even though they were in dire need of upgrades. He took pleasure in firing people for little or no valid reason, sometimes doing it the "day or two before" a major holiday (like Christmas, Thanksgiving, Fourth of July, New Year's, etc.) so he would not have to pay them holiday pay. He seldom paid vacation or personal time owed. If one of his preferred employees complained to him about the most insignificant issue, he would not hesitate to fire them. If he did not receive the fealty he felt he deserved, he would retaliate by making demeaning and derogatory comments about the employee.

Unfortunately, we also have many unethical failures who believe it is acceptable to steal from their own company, tarnishing the trust placed in them in the jobs they were hired for. One example of theft is a kickback: this occurs when a person negotiates a higher-than-market price for freight with a trucker, who is then paid the higher amount. Later, at a predetermined place and time, the embezzler is reimbursed by the trucker with the difference, usually in cash. This is illegal, and in one case, resulted in the offending managers being taken from their offices in handcuffs. Other unethical examples include: having a service provider build you a deck, replace your roof, pay for your son's summer basketball camp, or accepting trips, jewelry, or other valuable items. The opportunities for theft and corruption are endless.

If I could fire a warning shot to someone early in their business career, I would make it clear: avoid these corrupt individuals at all costs. We must focus on integrity during the hiring process. There are usually warning signs for people like this that we must not ignore. The above-noted examples by Pirates, who desecrate the dignity of workers, ruin careers, and steal from their own company, illustrate that these people thrive on such behavior.

It is also imperative to have a highly sophisticated and ethical financial auditing firm working with the Finance Team in your company. These auditing firms can electronically monitor and validate thousands of freight invoices daily, as well as provide reports that identify unusual variances and fraud. We should also avoid signing contracts with gain-share agreements that calculate weekly payments based on estimated cost savings or a percentage of the alleged cost savings. These agreements are often one-sided and not worth the paper they are written on. Most ethical auditing firms do not condone gain-share agreements anymore, because it is too easy for either party to steal. However, an ethical auditing firm is a great resource to identify and thwart illegal schemes. Sadly, there are unlimited ways to steal from a company, and professional Pirates lurk behind the blinds, waiting for their chance to pounce. Watch out for them, they are everywhere in business.

Chapter 13
Stairway to Heaven

"The greatest leaders mobilize others by coalescing people around a shared vision." - Ken Blanchard

Now at age 52, I had an excellent offer to join a large retailer in southwest Florida. It was a successful, family-owned company that had been in business for over 90 years and was going strong. The recruiter noted that it had a myriad of logistics-related problems, container detention, demurrage, high ocean, rail, trucking, and private fleet costs, that were significantly eroding sales. More importantly, my wife said that if I accepted the job, I would be heading to Florida without her. But I flew down to meet the key executives anyway, hoping her comment was in jest.

The upside was that the meetings went great, the location was beautiful, and the executives were sincere, down-to-earth, and looking for someone to fix their issues quickly. The downside was that the problems were immense. There were millions in unnecessary costs leaking from every mode of transportation, and there was pressure to fix them quickly. Plus, it was 1,500 miles away from my home in Massachusetts, but now both daughters were in college living in Boston, so the trauma of moving them was no longer an issue.

The job was appealing to me because I knew I could fix all these issues, but I needed the full support of everyone, from the Chairman of the Board to the DC dock associates. I requested this before I accepted the position and was told I had their full support. This included the possibility of having to replace some key positions with new, more knowledgeable, and collaborative managers. Some incumbent managers were deeply set in their ways, and there was no "teaching" opportunity here; the clock was running.

Ray and Dick, the SVP and COO respectively, were true to their word. They provided professional, personal, and financial support to me during my first six months on the job. They provided a nice apartment for me and continued that support until I sold my home in MA, even though I had exceeded the max limit. They allowed me to focus on my job and helped ensure that all of DC Operations listened to my strategies for improvement that required their help and execution. I was blessed with a large and talented staff who welcomed me and supported my ideas from Day One.

There were ten important initiatives that needed to be addressed quickly, but there was one that was deemed most important.

The company had paid several million in rail detention over the prior couple of years. My goal was to reduce this within the first three months. Detention is a penalty fee that we pay if we do not unload the rail container within the contract terms, which at the time was five days. In speaking with my new associates, it was clear that none of them were aware we had paid so much over the past two years. More importantly, most were not even aware of what detention was, let alone the calculation involved in determining the dollar amount.

My teaching skills were about to be tested. My very first week with the company, I held a daily class in our large DC conference room for distribution center supervisors and managers. I remember there being about 30 attendees from the Distribution Center, and about 10 were from my own staff. I taught them about what detention was, when the detention clock starts and stops, how it is calculated, and how unloading several thousand containers per year had deteriorated the bottom line of the company's profits. I asked them for their ideas and their commitment to eliminating it as soon as possible.

It was gratifying to see hands being raised to offer ideas on what they could do to expedite the process. Most in the room said they "had no idea" how much money we were losing, and I could feel some of them were bummed to learn that it was a "controllable" expense, not an uncontrollable one. The containers needed to be unloaded FIFO (first in, first out) to control detention. They had erroneously been told previously that containers should be worked randomly and not necessarily in order. The railroad had created this convoluted "averaging agreement" that was being misinterpreted, resulting in egregiously excessive detention payments.

I invited Dick and Ray to attend a meeting with the railroad to review the details of the averaging agreement. I believed the agreement was one-sided because it took the aggregate total of all containers, determined the dwell time, and multiplied those over five free days at $50 per day, per container. For example, if we unloaded 500 rail containers per month and averaged 10 days to unload versus their max of five, we would pay them

$250K per month. It did not give any credit for those unloaded in less than five days, so we negotiated a $50 (per day) credit offset for any container turned in less than five days. We also negotiated a start and stop clock. Detention would start on the date and time the container was dropped at our DC. The stop clock would trigger when we faxed the empty notification to the railroad. If it was prior to 12 noon, the detention clock would stop the same day; if sent after 12 noon, it would stop the following day. It was a big win for us because we had been paying whenever their trucker returned the empty to the rail head, which in some cases was more than three days after the fax notification.

Also, with the help of my IT-savvy Transportation Lead, we created a daily automated "Container Priority Report" that showed every container in the yard, how old it was, and the order in which it should be unloaded. The report updated every day and became the new bible for the Distribution Centers. They could not veer from this report if we wanted to eradicate detention.

We monitored our performance daily and could clearly see the FIFO process was working perfectly. We were creating a huge detention "credit" column, which was offsetting all detention. Within two months of my arrival, we eliminated detention. It was a huge achievement, and we celebrated by thanking the Distribution Centers with random cookouts and ice cream options. What a great feeling we all had after working collaboratively to achieve a very important corporate goal. Dick and Ray were really pleased. Unfortunately, railroads in today's world are not as receptive to negotiating free time as they were in the early 2000s.

The next initiative was changing the incumbent Ocean Forwarder to a better provider. We began negotiating directly with the ocean carriers to get significantly better rates and free time on ocean containers. The company had never negotiated directly with the ocean carriers, instead relying on the Forwarder, who had high rates and poor free time. Our container free time quickly went from about six days to 30 days by negotiating directly with the ocean carriers. This was another big win within the first five months of my arrival.

Within the first two years, we also renegotiated the LTL rates, the truckload rates, and the intermodal rail rates. In addition, we implemented a new TMS (Transportation Management System) that allowed us to automate the inbound routing process and simultaneously downsize our department. We shifted from faxes, phone calls, and emails to an automated system. We also transformed the Private Fleet delivery process by adopting a more cost-effective "floor loading" approach versus palletization, saving millions in the process by reducing the overall number of delivery trailers by about 35% while simultaneously increasing the number of cartons per outbound trailer. This operational enhancement allowed us to reallocate several of our Fleet Drivers to handle ocean and rail drayage rather than using third-party truckers for that service. It also provided better visibility into our domestic supply chain at the CSX railhead and the Port of Tampa, where we imported thousands of containers annually. After accomplishing all of these objectives, we still had more to do on our list.

This chapter is titled *Stairway to Heaven*, which, in my opinion, is the best rock song of all time. Released in 1971, I play it during my daily workout routine. It is a three-part, nine-minute journey, culminating in the final three minutes of unique artistic excellence in vocals, an amazing guitar riff, and percussion. It is impressively explosive as the tempo and volume rise proportionately over the nine-minute song, culminating in the finest combination of guitar (Jimmy Page), drums (John Bonham), and vocals (Robert Plant). With the drummer setting the pace like a conductor, his team follows his lead, resulting in a classic. The music leaves the listener in awe. To use a sports cliché: "they left it all on the floor." This team trusted each other to create a song that, 54 years later, is still considered one of the best rock songs of all time. Like Led Zeppelin, my team also "left it all on the floor."

I consider the execution, flow, and momentum of this song to be a metaphor for my own operational team members, who worked tirelessly to address every initiative with vigor and positivity. Each initiative had a high degree of complexity, yet our team worked diligently with focused precision. I applaud the efforts of Sue, Jason, Jeff, Tom, Hector, Tracy, and Leonard. The results of these efforts did not go unnoticed by Dick, Ray, and the other senior executives. In 2007, less than two years after arriving at this fine company, we were given the highest achievement in the company: The Chairman's Award. This award recognizes the most significant contribution to the company. As a leader in Logistics, it remains the proudest moment of my career to this day.

Our next challenges were to identify viable carrier options and open pool distribution operations at specific locations. This was needed to improve our DC-to-store throughput in our out-of-state locations. Keep in mind, these trailers had to be sorted and segregated by store prior to delivery. We selected North Carolina and Georgia as the preferred locations. We were able to successfully implement both locations within a 90-day period. This was another "best practice" and savings initiative. Shortly thereafter, we negotiated a new three-year UPS contract, saving millions, assisted in the implementation of a new e-commerce platform (HighJump), and converted our Private Fleet to a dedicated third-party fleet. We converted the fleet only after ensuring that all drivers would be hired and that their benefits would be equal to or better than what they had previously. The secondary benefit of doing this was to reduce the potential for unionization.

"Surround yourself with people that push you to do better. No drama or negativity. Just higher goals and higher motivation. Good times and positive energy. No jealousy or hate. Simply bringing out the absolute best in each other." - Warren Buffet.

After several years of professional success and achievement, both Dick and Ray retired, resulting in the usual changing of the guard. It is always a sad day when your biggest proponents leave and new people arrive with completely different ideas and perspectives. I stayed on for a couple of years after them but left when my youngest daughter was pregnant, in the third trimester with her first child. We wanted to be near her in Massachusetts, not 1,500 miles away in Southwest Florida. So, we made our final move to come home, this time for good.

It was a productive and enjoyable ten-year run, which I will always cherish. I am proud of the stellar accomplishments we achieved and the monetary contributions we were able to shift to the company's bottom line. Thanks especially to Dick and Ray for their unwavering support, and to my talented team, who worked side by side with me as we successfully executed every single initiative we were tasked with.

Chapter 14
Earning Respect and Public Speaking

"Before you are a leader, success is all about growing yourself. When you become a leader, success is all about growing others."
- Jack Welch

Between 2000 and 2019, I was highly visible in the logistics industry, holding Board of Director positions with CONECT (Coalition of N.E. Companies for Trade) and FTA (Florida Trucking Association), and speaking at many industry events, including RILA (Retail Industry Leaders Association), the TPM (Trans Pacific Maritime) conference, and several CONECT conferences. I was also requested to speak at six Florida Port conferences and wrote two executive op-eds for the *Journal of Commerce*. I was featured in *Supply Chain Magazine*'s Spring edition in 2014.

It was during this time frame that I met Peter, a senior executive and writer with the *Journal of Commerce*. Peter is unquestionably one of the most highly regarded global logistics experts in the world. I had read his insightful articles on international logistics for several years. We had a lot in common, including having graduated from the same university in New England. The *Journal of Commerce* is the bible of the global logistics field. It is a daily business journal with an array of outstanding writers and reporters who keep us all current in this ever-changing industry.

The JOC writers are successful because they interact directly with ocean carriers, forwarders, truckers, and railroads. Their information comes "from the horse's mouth," ensuring we receive accurate insights from high-level industry executives. Their expertise on tariffs, port congestion, equipment shortages, delays, and repositioning is invaluable. We rely on this daily information to provide timely insights to our own company executives and keep them aware of industry updates.

Peter asked me to lead a panel at their annual TPM Logistics Conference in Long Beach, and I agreed. It was an exciting experience, as Peter acted as the panel moderator.

For those of you with stage fright, join the club. I learned that very few executives openly embrace public speaking at a conference. My words of wisdom on this subject are twofold. First, the more frequently you speak in public, the better you become at it. More importantly, I learned that those in the audience want you to succeed. Attendees are a positive force; they want to hear your perspective and enjoy what you have to say. No one hopes you fail, in fact, it is quite the opposite. Knowing this makes it easier to succeed. In addition, as you grow in this dynamic field, you will inevitably have to speak in public at some point, so embrace it and try to enjoy it.

I found it helpful to accept an offer to speak or be on a panel a few months before the event. This lead time allowed me to relieve tension, knowing I had plenty of time to prepare. Conversely, accepting an invitation on short notice caused me to panic a couple of times. Be judicious when accepting invitations, and always ensure the topic aligns with your area of expertise rather than being entirely new to you.

Chapter 15
Best Practices is your Goal

"The first responsibility of a leader is to define reality. The last is to say Thank You." - Max Depree

Your corporate goal in Global Logistics is to ensure that "industry best practices" are being utilized by your company. It is difficult to be fully compliant because business rules change constantly in this dynamic field. It is important to stay informed by reading the *Journal of Commerce* daily newsletter. You can also read the information your carriers and forwarders provide weekly, and join industry organizations like NRF, CONECT, RILA, CSCMP, FDRA, etc. Accept every opportunity to join industry-related webinars, especially those that focus on specific issues pertinent to your organization. Most importantly, attend conferences to listen to industry experts, engage with your peers, and spend time with the hundreds of service providers. Each of the organizations noted above holds annual conferences; some have more than one. The TPM (Trans-Pacific Maritime) Conference, run by the *Journal of Commerce*, is the largest and usually takes place in early March in Long Beach, CA. It is well worth the time and money.

Every Logistics Department in the country should have all the answers below available and up to date to determine if you are using best practices. If not, it will help a Logistics expert make a thorough review and recommend efficiencies and cost savings. Having this information can help identify potentially millions of dollars in savings for a retailer:

- Where is the product made?

- How is it made, and what is it made of?

- Do you have an accurate HTS database for all current and prior items?

- Are repurposed or recycled fabrics being used?

- How many factories are there, and where are they located?

- How many factories are Fair Trade Certified?

- Are these partners' practices monitored and reviewed?

- Are both the factories and the importer of record (us) C-TPAT certified?

- How many units and packages are imported annually?

- How many units and packages are shipped annually?

- What are the primary inbound modes: ocean, air, LCL?

- What are your incoterms?

- What are the costs broken down by mode?

- What percentage of volume is handled by a forwarder?

- What percentage moves via direct ocean carrier contracts?

- What is the origin port pairing from which the product is imported?

- What are the destination US ports to which we are importing?

- How many ocean containers do we import annually in TEUs?

- Do you carry cargo insurance?

- What is the duty/tariff amount we pay by origin country?

- Where is the landed cost data for the past 12 months?

- Where are the destination distribution centers located?

- What are the operating hours of the DCs?

- Is there a YMS (Yard Management System)?

- Can containers be dropped, or is it a live appointment operation?

- Is the facility union or non-union?

- Are the employees company employees or leased labor?

- Is it an automated or manual facility?

- How many orders/packages can be received and shipped daily?

- What is the percentage of returns?

- Do you outsource returns or handle them in-house?

- What is the WMS (Warehouse Management System) being used?

- What are the delivery modes: Small Parcel, LTL, TL, Air, Pool Distribution?

- What TMS (Transportation Management System) or shipping platform do you use?

- Does the DC utilize sustainable and eco-friendly packaging?

Once you have all the information noted above, an assessment can be made of best practices, C-TPAT certifications, yard operational improvements, throughput gains, and, most importantly, cost savings opportunities. If you have not conducted a Logistics Departmental reassessment in 2 to 3 years, consider doing one now. This is especially important for those with a heavy reliance on UPS and FedEx small package services. Those contracts are usually over 20 pages long and written with the intent to confuse the customer. Make sure you have the in-house talent to decipher these contracts and renegotiate them to your benefit when contractually feasible. Otherwise, consider hiring a knowledgeable industry consultant who specializes in small package contracts to provide insight and focus on where the savings opportunities are.

Chapter 16
The Fighter Pilot

"A true leader has the has the confidence to stand alone, the courage to make tough decisions, and the compassion to listen to the needs of others." - General Douglas McArthur

Now, at age 63, I had just spent the previous 12 months dealing with a serious health issue, which was both time-consuming and physically draining. It took a lot out of me, and I was away from the workforce, as my system had a tough time recovering from 44 radiation treatments. As soon as I healed, I considered returning to the workforce but knew it would be an uphill battle due to my age and health.

I applied for a few local positions so I could return to work. I had watched ageism from a distance through several colleagues and expected to see the same in my quest for a new job. I have always found it baffling that the most knowledgeable and mature executives are often overlooked in favor of a younger, less knowledgeable person. In my business of Global Logistics, companies need expertise and someone who can identify and turn a bad situation around quickly. They do not need a 40-year-old if their problems will not be identified and resolved efficiently. The truly talented logistics executives can save their salaries several times over by lowering ocean, air, trucking, UPS, and FedEx contracts.

I met Jimmy (my last Tugboat) in the fall of 2017. He was a highly decorated (retired) Lieutenant Colonel in the US Air Force. His resume was littered with awards and medals, and he had flown about six different aircraft, including the Stealth Bomber. He was the SVP of Operations and Logistics for a retailer with multiple fulfillment centers specializing in e-commerce. Although his office was only 30 minutes from my home, he asked me to fly to Kansas to meet him and other key managers. Not thrilled with the request, I still flew to Kansas for the first time in my life to meet Jimmy.

I had imagined meeting a strict, formal, dictatorial executive because of his military background. Instead, I met the most engaging, affable, and approachable senior executive I had ever encountered in my career. He was also very "driven" and had operational issues that required my expertise. At no point did I feel uncomfortable about my age. In fact, there were two others on the interviewing team who appeared to be older. Jimmy wanted expertise and someone he could trust to fix logistics issues without having to look over his shoulders. We hit it off immediately, and I started with him a few days later. The biggest issues were international, specifically China and Taiwan, where most of our products were sourced. I made several trips to Asia during my time with him.

We quickly addressed a diverse number of global logistics issues. We changed our global forwarder, added more cost-effective ocean carriers with "direct contracts," and successfully renegotiated our small package rates, which significantly reduced our e-commerce budget. We documented all the savings and efficiencies we proudly achieved together.

Our new international forwarder was owned by Pat, a Boston native with a highly committed staff of professionals. Pat and I traveled a few times to Asia (Shanghai, Ningbo, Kaohsiung, Taichung, etc.) to expand our use of buyers' consolidation at origin.

We also visited the headquarters of his international partner in Shanghai and spent time with the Managing Director. The visits paid dividends as capacity disappeared during Peak Season, and thousands of importers were unable to move their cargo from Asia to the US unless they paid ten times the normal ocean rate. Ocean carriers were ripping up their existing contracts with customers. Not only did Pat and his partner come through for us, we never paid a dime above what we had contractually agreed with them. This was unheard of in the industry, especially for a low-volume importer.

When Peak ended, I asked Pat what motivated him to keep his word and not increase our rates when all other forwarders and carriers in the industry did. He responded: "We are in this business for the long haul, not one year. We committed to help you succeed, and we kept our promise." We awarded him our 2018 Logistics Provider of the Year award as recognition. Honoring your commitment is the norm for truly ethical companies. Always seek out companies like this to have in your carrier base. Always check their websites to see how they give back to their communities. That information is a great resource to help judge carriers when receiving bids and comparing one against another.

As of this writing, at 71, I am finishing up my final Global Logistics project. I am appreciative of the time Jimmy and I had together. We remain friends, and I will always treasure his support and receptivity when I joined him. Jimmy was blind to ageism, focusing only on talent and expertise. Of all the qualities we discussed in this book, these could be the most important: "Respect" and "Honoring Your Commitment" to others.

"We must find time to stop and thank those people who made a difference in our lives." – John F. Kennedy

In closing, I would like to convey my appreciation to all my colleagues, Captains, and Crewmembers. I am thankful for the mutual trust and respect we all showed one another during my forty years in retail logistics. I especially want to convey my heartfelt thanks to my seven most significant mentors, who were my most supportive influencers. My Tugboats are as follows:

- Bob, the calming professional who taught me very early in my career about building a quality team while introducing me to computers when they were in their infancy. I am forever thankful that he recommended me for promotion twice in a four-year period, pushing my young career in the right direction.

- Charlie, the brilliant teacher and tactician who took me under his wing and helped me learn and grow as a leader in Logistics. He provided me with a lifelong business lesson as we filed for Chapter 11 bankruptcy but emerged from it shortly thereafter, with our business continuing through the process.

- Dave, the ethical leader who showed me the importance of communicating through positive reinforcement and always making the effort to bring out the best in others. He not only talked the talk; he walked the walk. Dave treated everyone with dignity and respect and expected the same from his team toward others.

- Greg, the voice of reason in my life when my career was at a crossroads. He went out of his way to help me find the right path and also supported my promotion to Vice President shortly after my arrival at his company. He was a strong proponent of mine both during our time together and later in my career.

- Dick and Ray, whose generosity and commitment during my transition from Massachusetts to Florida were humbling. They also provided unwavering professional support to my team and me as we were tasked with an unending list of very difficult projects. We would not have achieved them without their full support.

- Jimmy, the highly decorated retired Lt. Colonel in the Air Force who enthusiastically embraced me at an age when most others would not. Our many business successes, both domestic and international, were attributable to our mutual trust and respect for each other.

The Tugboat Leadership Compass:

North – Purpose: Know why you lead. Tugboats guide others toward a shared destination, not personal glory.

East – Mentorship: Lift others through teaching and trust. All good leaders are lifelong learners and mentors.

South – Integrity: Ethics and humility matter more than speed or power.

West – Teamwork: Move in harmony with your crew. Success in logistics and leadership is never solo.

Center – Gratitude: Remember the people who helped you reach calm waters.

Epilogue

This book is dedicated to my dearest friends in business. Special thanks to my seven personal Tugboats for your commitment and the professional guidance I received throughout my career. Additional thanks to my Captains and Crewmembers for providing me with the impetus to write this book. I am forever grateful to you, it was a wild and productive ride.

Thank you also to my family for providing me with unending support, especially when relocating was necessary, helping me achieve my business-related goals.

Thanks, and God bless each of you.

Bob Kamel, Charlie Messina, Dave Gary, Greg Diefenbach, Dick Judd, Ray Gordon, Jimmy Donohue, Scooch Giargiari, Tom Dromey, Russ Aborn, Fred Snyder, Peter Tirshwell, Ted Lepcio, Gary Lawrence, John Firmin, Ron Marotta, Naoya Endo, Irene Tung, Ken Kellaway, David McLaughlin, Pay Fay, Frank Martell, John Rynearson, Paula Dudley, Tom Shafer, Sue Miller, Jason Smith, Jeff Marsteller, Paul Cook, Tracy H, Tony Gordon, Steve Carr, Mike M., Lenard Ivory, Jim Mitchell, Dan Wolf, Joni Padduck, Harold Goodman, Charlie Mangini, Lindsay Shumlas, Michael Jacobs, Heather Freeman.

About The Author

For more than 40 years in global logistics, Rich Higgins has guided teams through change, challenge, and success. Embracing the belief that real leadership starts with teaching and teamwork, he has assisted organizations through mergers, turnarounds, and international sourcing expansions. He was a board member for CONECT and the Florida Trucking Association and was also featured in *Supply Chain World* magazine. He has been a speaker and panelist at several industry conferences, including RILA, TPM, CONECT, and ITTS in Tampa. Rich and his wife, Becky, live in Shrewsbury, MA.